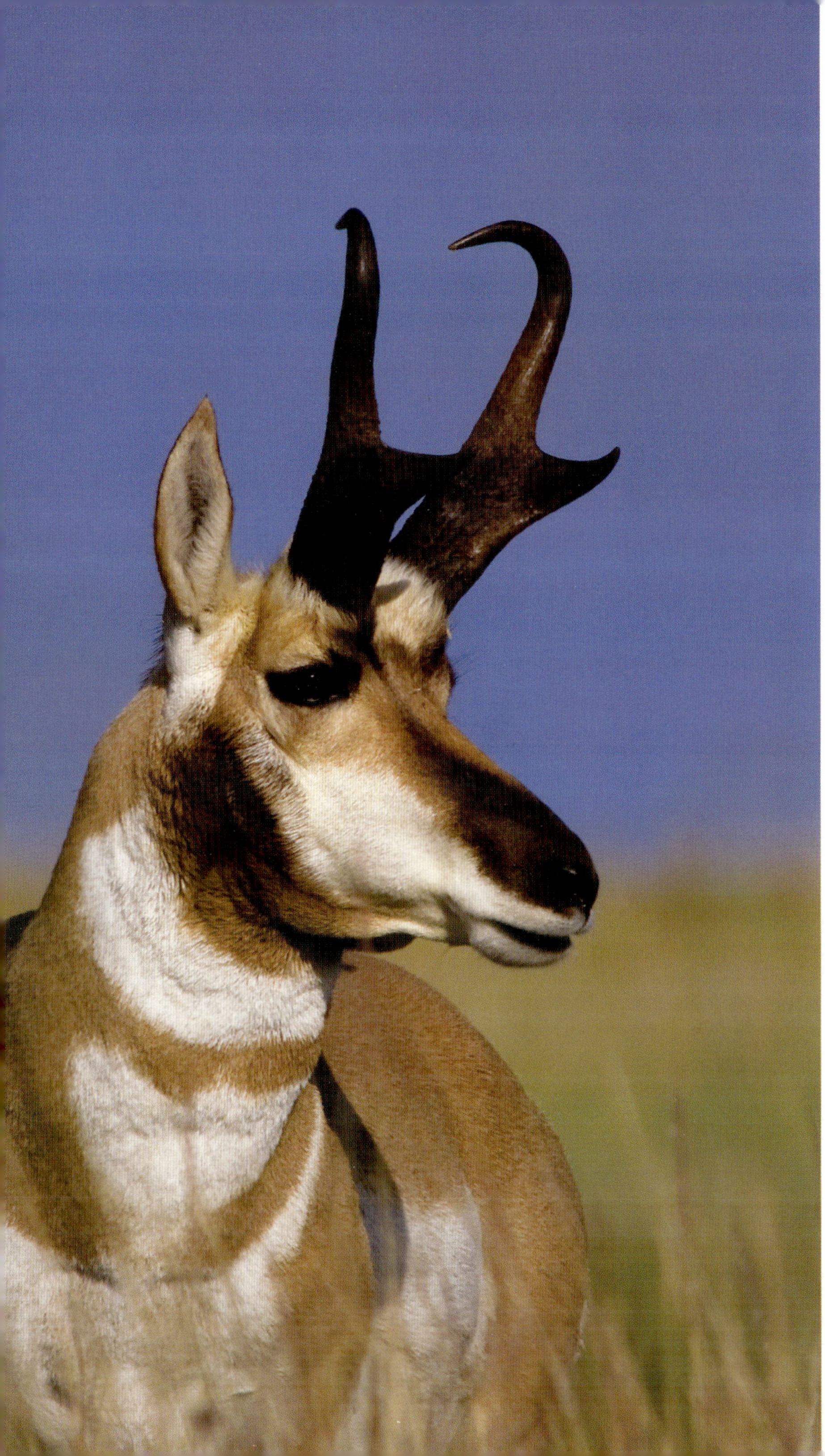

A Pronghorn Year

a visual tribute to North America's pronghorn

Photography & Text by Dick Kettlewell

A nursing doe stops for a long drink before returning to her fawns to attend their needs.

*To my
wonderful wife Joan,
who helps me see
the possibilities.*

ISBN 10: 1-56037-601-5 | ISBN 13: 978-1-56037-601-9

For more information about our books, write Farcountry Press, P.O. Box 5630, Helena, MT 59604; call (800) 821-3874; or visit www.farcountrypress.com.

Library of Congress Cataloging-in-Publication Data
Kettlewell, Dick.
  A pronghorn year : a visual tribute to North America's pronghorn.
    pages cm
  ISBN 978-1-56037-601-9 -- ISBN 1-56037-601-5
1. Pronghorn. 2. Pronghorn--Pictorial works. I. Title.
  QL737.U52K48 2014
  599.63'9--dc23

                              2014004801

Created, produced, and designed in the United States.

Printed in China.

18 17 16 15 14   1 2 3 4 5

Table of Contents

*(above) Sibling fawns, a buck and doe, poke through the midsummer grass that is
fast filling with tasty wildflowers and other shrubs.*

*(cover) As autumn gives way to winter on the high plains, pronghorn gather into mixed age
and gender groups that include mature bucks and does along with last summer's fawns.*

Introduction

An old legend of the Blackfoot explains how the pronghorn came to be on the prairies.

After the land was made, Old Man or Na'pi—who was God the creator to the Blackfoot—traveled about on it, making things and fixing up the Earth so as to suit him. First he marked out places where he wished the rivers to run, sometimes making them run smoothly or putting falls and rapids on them in other places. He made the prairies, created the tall timbers of the forests along with the small trees and bushes, and sometimes carried rocks with him from which he built mountains.

Old Man caused the grass to grow on the plains so that the animals might have something on which to feed. He marked off certain pieces of land where he made places for the camas, wild carrots, wild turnips, sweet root and bitterroot, serviceberries, bull berries, cherries, plums, and rosebuds.

Yes, Old Man was meticulous and possessed great imagination, but he didn't always get things right the first time and sometimes had to correct mistakes as he went along.

During his time among the forests on the stony slopes of the mountains, he made the pronghorn out of dirt and turned it loose to see how it would go.

But Ho! Old Man was very disappointed. Here the animal's great speed was a hindrance. Among the trees were fallen timbers and rocks that caused him to stumble and trip. His fabulous eyesight was of little use in the thick forests where he could only see the trees that were right in front of him. Hidden predators easily ambushed him.

Old man lamented his mistake, but knew what to do as he moved his creation to the prairies. Here the pronghorn's wondrous speed carried him like the wind away from cunning predators like the wolf and coyote. His huge eyes detected the smallest speck and the slightest motion across the rolling grasslands and endless vistas. Here he has flourished and done very well ever since.

The pleasant words of allegorical narratives like this one may oversimplify just a bit why an animal adapts to or with a particular environment or ecosystem on our planet. But this legend clearly demonstrates how well the Blackfoot understood why the pronghorn and the prairies are as one.

Yes, the elk may be more regal and certainly the bison is a more widely accepted symbol of the American West. And yet this animal we call the antelope or pronghorn may be the most remarkable creature of an ecosystem that abounds with remarkable creatures.

He is the Prince of the Prairie.

(above) A pronghorn doe prances down a prairie slope shortly after dawn on a South Dakota summer's morning.

(facing page) A product of Earth's most recent ice age, the pronghorn is still a staple sight on the prairies of North America and exists nowhere else on our planet.

Born for the Prairies

(above) A pronghorn buck wanders through the grass below a dawn sky along Boland Ridge in South Dakota's Wind Cave National Park.

(left) The Lame Johnny Creek Basin of South Dakota's Custer State Park is home to prairie grasses, plants, shrubs, and flowers, ideal pronghorn country. High points for visual scanning in all directions are abundant, along with deep ravines that provide protection from winter's icy winds. The meandering creek, with its deep pools that still hold water even during dry years, runs deep throughout the basin in wet ones. And of course there's room to run.

A group of does dashes across a prairie ridge choked with purple coneflowers during a midsummer evening. The sole living remnant of an ancient family of goats from Asia called Antilocapridae, the pronghorn as we know them are believed to have evolved in North American during the Pleistocene epoch.

A League of Its Own

The picture of grace! Dancers all. Watching a line of pronghorn prance across the prairie may not compare with the Bolshoi Ballet, but it's a pretty good second.

No other creature captures the essence of the North American prairies in the way that the American pronghorn does. Here is the quintessential animal of an ecosystem that features climatic extremes: harsh winters, baking summers, torrential thunderstorms, and frequent droughts.

Pronghorns are simply beautiful. The extraordinary coloration of their heads—the light tans contrasting with the jet black of their noses and snowy white cheek patches—is unequaled for visual resplendence. Watch the dawn light accent those great, high horns that adorn the head of a mature buck. See him stand erect as the sun's glint catches in his huge dark eyes that can detect the slightest movement in the midst of a vast prairie landscape. It is perfection witnessed.

Is it an antelope . . . or a pronghorn? And what's the difference? The first European explorers of the American West dubbed this creature an antelope because it seemed similar to the antelope species they had seen in Africa and Asia. And they knew of nothing else to which it compared.

Both names—antelope and pronghorn—have come to be accepted, although this creature is neither a true antelope nor a member of the deer family, as others believe. More closely related to goats, the pronghorn has evolved entirely in North America.

Paleontologists believe that the pronghorn's ancestors—several species of goats or goat-like creatures—migrated across the Bering land bridge from Asia about 20 million years ago. Grouped in an ancient taxonomic family called Antilocapridae, these animals ranged from what are now the Canadian prairies to as far south as the Floridian peninsula and Mexico.

(above) A mature buck relaxes in the midsummer grass. Unlike other ungulates, a pronghorn's horns actually point backward, rising straight up and then curving toward the rump.

(above) A territorial buck trots leisurely through a prairie ravine in late summer on a routine patrol of his ground. Pronghorn have made running an art; field biologists have documented thirteen different gaits, from the "very slow diagonal walk" to the "lateral gallop." Many zoologists believe that the existence of a North American cheetah before the start of the last ice age is one of the reasons that pronghorn developed their tremendous speed. Today's pronghorn may actually be a bit slower because this cheetah, thus the predator pressure, no longer exists.

Bearing little likeness to the creature we know today, they came in many shapes and sizes to a North America that was more reminiscent of central Africa. This North America was rich in savannah-like ecosystems and supported many species of large mammals—especially predators—spread almost entirely across the continent.

Among them were the saber-toothed cat, the dire wolf, and the short-faced bear, along with an American lion similar in appearance to the African lion of today, and an American cheetah as well. Many of these predators were considerably larger than any similar species today. The short-faced bear, for example, was nearly twice the size of the present-day grizzly bear.

Herbivores and ungulates included a giant ground sloth and long-horned bison, as well as today's familiar bison, camels, native horses, and even pachyderms like the mastodon and woolly mammoth.

This world would soon change, as the ice ages of the Pleistocene Epoch extended their massive glacial sheets southward from the polar cap across nearly half of the northern hemisphere. Toward the end of the Pleistocene, most of those ancient North American mammals became extinct.

(above) Like this doe, at high speeds most pronghorn move with their mouths gaping. This is not from exhaustion, but to allow their large respiratory system to process oxygen at the extraordinary rate of 6 to 10 liters per minute–five times the capacity of any similarly sized mammals. A larger supply of hemoglobin also transports more oxygen from the lungs to the muscles, providing more power.

(left) Pronghorn are also well adapted to summer heat. After molting to a thinner coat, they are able to erect their body hair, allowing body heat to dissipate during exertion. Although young bucks like these usually reach sexual maturity by the age of one year, they generally don't have much opportunity to breed until they are around three years old.

Those various species of goats either adapted or were eliminated until finally one animal emerged—not quite a goat anymore, nor was it like any other animal on this planet. It was a highly social being with a large brain capable of adaptability and learning, a creature perfectly suited for life on the North American prairies: *Antilocapra americana.*

The most remarkable characteristics of the American pronghorn—certainly those that have contributed most to its success on the prairies—are its speed and vision.

It is the fastest land animal in North America and second only to the African cheetah throughout the world, having been clocked at speeds of sixty-eight miles per hour. While the cheetah is quicker during initial bursts and short sprints, the pronghorn would pull ahead after about a hundred yards and continue at the same speed for a much longer distance.

If such an event as an animal track meet could be held, the cheetah would probably take the 100-meter dash, but the pronghorn would own the 440 and 880. These amazing athletes can hold a pace of thirty-eight to forty miles per hour for as far as seven miles, making them the world's champion distance runners.

And neither do they lack for agility, being able to cut and dodge at angles that would make them the envy of any NFL running back. This speed is, of course, the pronghorn's first line of defense—it simply leaves any other animal choking in its dust.

(left) This large, dominant buck proudly displays a rack that approaches perfection. Notice the rich heart-shaped curve in the horns rising about fourteen inches above his head from a base of nearly three inches. The prongs or "paddles" extend about two inches out from the horns that are finally adorned with ivory-colored tips.

(below) A pronghorn's strong herd instinct hinges on an advanced social order and status ranking, which are maintained with subtle glances, vocalizations, and body language. This keeps conflicts to a minimum so that the herd's focus is solely on the trials of survival on the prairie.

In praise of the Prince

(above) Pronghorn feed selectively, consuming mostly shrubs and forbs, with grasses being a minor part of their diet. By using her dexterous upper lips to draw and hold plant parts with her mouth while cutting them free with her incisors, this doe does not uproot the buffalo clover on which she is feeding and the plant continues to grow. This easy manner of grazing, coupled with the fact that they eat many plants that other wildlife and livestock will not touch, is yet another example of how well adapted the pronghorn is to its prairie environment.

As for their vision, some have likened it to that of a human using a pair of eight-power binoculars. While that comparison would be difficult to confirm, make no mistake: the pronghorn's vision is exceptional and a very effective early warning device. Nothing sneaks up on these guys.

The pronghorn's eyes, about two inches in diameter, are similar in size to those of an African elephant. Set high on the side of the head, these protuberant eyes also give them the advantage of a nearly 360-degree field of vision.

Watch pronghorn graze and you will notice them looking up periodically to scan their surroundings with that fixed stare to a distant horizon. After a time, you may be able to pick out the speck of an approaching rival or a coyote sizing up its chances to close the gap.

(above) By mid-November, bucks like this one begin shedding the outer keratin sheaths we see most of the year, exposing the inner bone core that is a permanent part of their skull.

(right) This young buck scans across the horizon before returning to the business of feeding and ruminating. His disproportionately large and protuberant eyes can spot the movement of an approaching predator or rival from as far as three miles away. And with those eyes located far back on their head, they can keep watch even while the head is down during feeding.

(above) Pronghorn have a four-chambered stomach and, like most herbivores, they digest their food twice. After the food first passes through the stomach, they regurgitate it and chew it again, breaking the plant material into smaller pieces for greater nutrient absorption. Also, a proportionately larger liver removes from the bloodstream plant toxins that are dangerous to other ungulates.

Still other factors contribute to the pronghorn's survival. It regularly eats whatever is available, including shrubs and weeds that other species, short of starvation, will not touch. More than 400 plants fall into the pronghorn diet, including clover, wild onion, lupine, dandelion, mustard, sagebrush, saltbush, bitterbrush, cheatgrass, and bluegrass. Also, pronghorn can go long periods without water and even survive on the moisture content of foliage if need be.

Their style of grazing is also easy on the land. Unlike many other animals that grab a mouthful of a plant and uproot it entirely, a pronghorn bites off small portions and leaves the rest of the plant still rooted in the ground. Pronghorn regularly consume weeds such as cockleburs and thistles that are considered a scourge by most ranchers.

One important taxonomic characteristic of a true antelope, such as the African animal, is that its horns are hollow, unbranched, and permanent—not shed on a seasonal basis.

The horn of the American pronghorn is branched, just barely. Halfway up the main horn a small projection or prong extends to the front, thus the name "pronghorn."

Part of their headgear is solid; part of it is not. The outer sheath is hollow and composed of keratin, the same hair-like protein substance as a cat's claws and our fingernails. Beneath the sheath is a shiny inner core that is bone and permanent.

The pronghorn does shed its horns, but not entirely. Following the autumn rut, the hollow sheath, which we see most of time, is shed to reveal the solid inner core, usually by late November. Over the winter, the sheath grows back, with the cycle complete by early spring. Unlike the buck, the pronghorn doe has only small projections on her head, if at all, most of which are bone and are not shed.

(above) During wet years on the prairie, creeks and ponds like this one are full and available all across the grasslands for animals like these pronghorn does. Come drier years, the pronghorn derive most of their water from the plants they eat.

(below) Pronghorn are first and foremost creatures of the herd. Except for a brief period of a few weeks during the autumn rut when bucks like these two defend a territory or harem against intrusion and theft, these animals live in some type of a cooperative or social group. These gatherings vary from mixed gender and age groups in winter to bachelor groups of young bucks in spring or does with fawns forming "day-care" groups in summer.

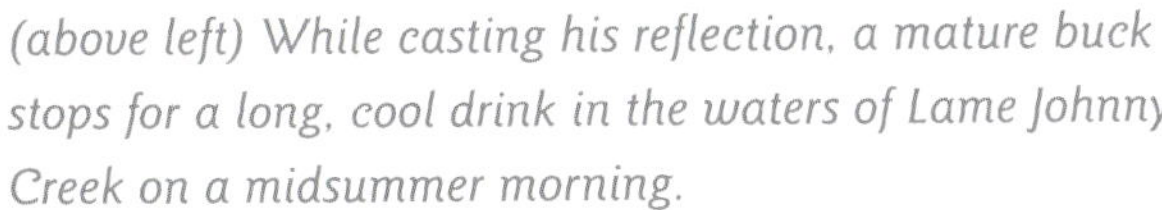

(above left) While casting his reflection, a mature buck stops for a long, cool drink in the waters of Lame Johnny Creek on a midsummer morning.

(above right) Forbs are typically non-woody flowering plants like this western salsify. They are the mainstay of the pronghorn's summer diet.

(right) The nutritional value of those forbs is critical to the does and the birth of healthy fawns, like this little buck playing in the mid-June grass.

Another deceiving characteristic of the pronghorn is its size. When seeing them up close for the first time, many people are surprised that this animal is not larger. Most people see them only from a distance and even then usually just their white rumps disappearing over a far ridge. In the vastness of the prairie landscape we rarely have anything to which we can compare them and get a better sense of their true size.

The average buck weighs about 120 pounds, with a shoulder height of 30 to 33 inches—about the height of a typical desk or table. The biggest bucks top out at about 140 pounds. Does are about the same height as bucks but lighter at 100 to 105 pounds.

I once heard the writer Dan O'Brien remark, "Those pronghorn are one animal that just doesn't get much respect or attention . . . seems like they deserve better." True enough.

I am sometimes amazed at how little is known or understood about this remarkable animal even by people who live in the West and see them often. On the big game hunters' popularity list the pronghorn is a distant fifth, with bighorn sheep, elk, mule deer, and white-tailed deer far ahead.

Yet this creature comes to us from another time in the life of our Earth. Think of it. While many well-established species were unable to survive the Pleistocene epoch, the most cataclysmic geological event of recent Earth history, these animals actually evolved through the midst of that event, as though they did so on the run just ahead of the advancing ice. Now that's performance under pressure.

I think the pronghorn has more than earned our "respect and attention."

(left) Come spring, pregnant does like this one usually isolate themselves to give birth. When the fawns are a few weeks old, the fawns and mothers integrate into doe-fawn or daycare groups where security in numbers comes into play.

(above) The herd serves as an instrument of survival in an ecosystem where seclusion is next to impossible. Groupings like this one provide many individuals that can alternate from scanning the distance for predators to feeding. Also, each can sound an alarm with a wheezing, almost bird-like call that is unmistakable in its sound. And the group itself enhances each individual's survival chances: a predator can only bring down one animal at a time while the others escape. Some of the pronghorn's herding tendencies are really an adaptation to the predator presence of another time, against predators that no longer exist. With rare exceptions, healthy adults are seldom victims of predation nowadays. But they don't know that yet.

(above) The pronghorn's speed is remarkable in two ways. First, it has been clocked flat out at about sixty-eight miles per hour, easily making it North America's fastest land animal. But second and even more astounding, this creature can maintain speeds of thirty-five to forty miles per hour over a distance of eight miles, even up steep hills and down deep ravines. They would complete a twenty-six-mile marathon course in about forty minutes, whereas the best human runner needs more than two hours.

(facing page) As these two does dash through the tall summer grass, their exceptional eyesight is also a benefit in helping them to spot hidden boulders and other possible obstacles. Anatomical features contributing to the pronghorn's running ability include strong but slender limbs with forelegs in which the bones are light and disproportionately long. Its heart, lungs, and windpipe are much larger than those of any other comparably sized animal to increase air intake. A larger carotid artery keeps the brain cooled more effectively during these extreme exertions. The pronghorn is a running machine.

(above) With the hairs of her white rump patch flared in the typical manner that denotes alarm, this doe races away through a prairie meadow. Their feet are pointed double hooves with cartilage padding that cushions the shock of running over hard ground and rocks. Most of their weight is carried on the front hooves, which are larger than the back. Glands on each foot secrete an oily conditioner for the hooves. With legs that are built more for running than jumping, these animals do have a marked preference for going under things like range fences, something they never encountered until about 125 years ago. However, some members of more recent generations have taken to jumping over the shorter fences, another sign of their remarkable ability for adaptation.

(left) On cue from this doe, these three fawns
take off with her through the tall grass on
a late summer's morning after she spots an
approaching coyote. Many biologists believe
that the average doe is actually a bit faster
than most bucks. And the fact that pronghorn
are overwhelmingly faster than any predator
that exists today also leads researchers to
believe that their speed is another adaptation
from a previous time when North American
fauna featured many more predators that were
considerably larger and faster than any found
on today's prairies.

(above) Pronghorn are to the North American prairies what caribou are to the Arctic tundra or giraffes are to the African Serengeti: an animal that doesn't just make do with its surroundings, but has become one with them. They personify the prairie, which would be a vacuous place without them.

(left) To many, the prairie is desolate, boring and empty—probably so if all you ever see of it is interstate highways and truck stops. But take an early morning walk through the ravines and over the rolling hills as the dawn light creeps across the grass and the experience is absolutely primal.

Season of the Fawns

(above) Multiple births among pronghorn are typical. These buck and doe siblings, now four to five weeks old, will continue to nurse at least another month while also feeding on the rich forbs and shrubs that now bloom all across the prairie. By summer's end both fawns will have developed the stamina and locomotive skills necessary for the legendary fleetness of their species.

(left) Shortly after a dawn rainfall. this doe and her fawn, about forty-eight hours old, enjoy a playful moment of bonding in South Dakota's Custer State Park. On the northern prairies most fawns are born during a five- to six-week period from late May to the end of June.

(above) Curled with ears down flat against its neck, this buck fawn remained completely motionless though I inadvertently walked to within several inches of him before finally noticing him. He never moved a muscle while I shot several frames of him with a 24mm lens. Acting out the first stage of what biologists call "the hiding strategy," which is designed to protect young from predators, the fawn will spend about ten days in pure hiding except for periodic visits from his mother for care and feeding. Notice how he actually bears resemblance to the lump of dried buffalo chips beside him, giving further evidence of the stealthy skills employed by pronghorn young as they disappear into the wide-open prairie.

The First Fawn

The wily little doe ambled on ahead through the dense prairie shrubbery, stopping periodically to glance back at me or to shake off the pesky flies that are a constant this time of year.

Slowly dropping her head, she began to munch at the grass around her. Then, with equal calculation, she suddenly rose up, turned about, and threw a long hard stare in the far distance to my left.

She was still pretty young, but already worldly wise in every trick known to her species. I knew it was unlikely that anything lay in the direction she faced and that she was just "looking me off." The phrase is a football term referring to when the quarterback, as he retreats to pass, looks away with exaggeration from the primary receiver—hoping to mislead the defensive backs in their pursuit of the play.

"Clever, clever," I thought.

For nearly two hours now I had watched that unmistakable style in her body language: prolonged stares to a distant ridge; quick glances back over the shoulder, first at me and then beyond. Occasionally she would break into a trot, covering maybe thirty yards, and then stop to begin the cycle again, always moving in a circular pattern over several hundred yards.

This doe had a secret.

Somewhere in the endless sea of grass surrounding me was new and vulnerable life awaiting the return of motherly care—one or maybe even two newborn fawns. The doe's behavior was part of that motherly care. The meandering stares and encircling routine were all designed to lead me away from her secret in the grass.

I had been crouched in the same spot for about ten minutes now when I realized the doe had changed her pattern. She would stare

(below) Typically, newborn fawns like this one weigh 5 to 7 pounds, stand about 8 to 10 inches at the shoulder, and are all legs. During the final days of pregnancy, a pronghorn mother will move off by herself to a site where she will birth her fawns. Site selection is critical because the limited mobility of the fawns will confine both them and the doe to a comparatively small area for the next two weeks as the hiding phase begins.

(below) Every two to four hours throughout the day, this little buck's mother will return from grazing nearby to feed him. Known as the reunion period, this time lasts five to ten minutes, with the doe bedding the fawn again about 100 yards or so from this spot. She is especially alert during this period because the fawn is highly visible and easily spotted by predators. After about ten to twelve days with the fawn staying completely hidden, there is a slow transition from hiding, and these reunion periods last an hour or more. This little one was probably born during the previous night. Like this doe, most adult pronghorn approach the peak of the spring molt or shedding period in late May.

right at me and then lift her head to look beyond. "Could it be...?" I thought. I began to scan my immediate surroundings.

Incredible! No more than two feet from the toe of my boot was a buck fawn curled in the typical circular posture with his ears down flat against his neck, perfectly still. Born during the night, he'd been there all the time and had done absolutely nothing to give away his position. I could have tripped over him.

Few animals possess the stealth of a pronghorn fawn. They can hide behind a blade of grass. At birth they lack the trademark and striking pelage of the adults and are instead a non-descript grayish brown, with their hair running in curly waves. That brilliant, distinctive white rump patch is a subdued yellow. In fact, lying curled like this one today, he bore a striking resemblance in shape and color to the buffalo chip beside him.

His genius for camouflage and his mother's discretion will be this little guy's chief allies during the next five or six weeks as he, barely out of the womb, enters this most critical period known as the hiding phase. Like this morning, he will spend hours at a time lying flat and motionless in such a way as to blend perfectly into his prairie environment.

The fawn most likely had a sibling, as multiple births are very common among pronghorn. If so, the doe will keep the two bedded separately, thereby enhancing the odds that at least one will survive this critical period. She will visit each one periodically throughout the day to nourish their seven-pound frames with some of the richest milk known on this planet—more than twice the protein and three times the fat of cow's milk.

Nurtured by this milk, his young spindly legs which now lack stamina will grow, develop, and soon carry the youngster across the prairie at speeds of more than sixty miles per hour, leaving swift predators like the coyote far behind.

I glanced back at his mother. She seemed to realize I had spotted the baby as she took a few steps toward me and then stopped to

(above) On her feet when she was barely twenty minutes old, this little doe at four days of age can now easily outrun a man, though she will still lack the stamina necessary to distance herself from swift predators like the coyote until she's eight to ten weeks old. Contributing to the fawn's rapid development is its long gestation period of 252 days—considerably longer than several larger animals like mule deer (196 days) or bighorn sheep (180 days).

(above) During most of their first two weeks, these sibling fawns will see very little of each other as their mother keeps them bedded separately, increasing the chance that at least one will survive the summer. About twenty-four hours old, these fawns together constitute about eighteen percent of their mother's weight. A human female giving birth to twins at that percentage of her weight would have babies weighing more than twelve pounds each.

cast a wary eye, though she didn't really seem upset. Stressing her was the last thing I wanted to do, so I needed to move away as soon as I could.

I rose up slowly. Using a camera with a wide-angle lens, I fired off several frames of the fawn as he lay still. Then I grabbed the rest of my gear, carefully moved off, and crouched down again about thirty yards or so away.

I knew if I were patient enough, sooner or later the doe would get the toddler up for feeding and care, giving me great pictures of interaction between mother and child.

For another hour the doe continued to browse for food, circling around me. And then it all came together. She suddenly trotted straight over to where the little buck lay and he stood up instantly to greet his mother. As I quickly focused on the two, I heard a bleating sound similar to a baby lamb or goat. Thirty yards or so to their right, the twin, a doe, stood up in tall shrubs and stumbled over to her mother and little brother.

Perfect.

We all have our own ways of marking the passage of time, ways in which we chronicle and catalog the events around us as well as those of our own lives. For many Native American cultures it was observing the moon's cycles or the keeping of a winter count.

For me, it is the coming of the pronghorn fawns. Every year in late May or early June, I anxiously anticipate my first sighting and note the day on which it happens. I consider them to be among the most beautiful creatures on our planet. Who couldn't love those huge and gorgeous eyes, their lovable expressions of curiosity, the antics of their play with one another.

This day begins the Season of the Fawns.

(below) The hiding strategy requires coordinated behavior between mother and fawn. After the mother selects a new bedding site, the fawn will move off ten to fifteen yards to a reclining spot without the doe following so that she does not leave a scent that predators can trace to the young one. Zoologist John Byers has described this strategy as "an elaborate shell game played with coyotes."

(below) This nursing doe stands vigil from a ridgetop overlooking a large prairie creek basin where she has twin fawns stashed separately in the grass, probably as much as 100 yards apart. She will move in a meandering circular pattern around the basin while watching over the youngsters, employing great care and strategy not to give away their position. Pronghorn does are not merely passive in their efforts to protect fawns; they are known to attack predators like coyotes using their sharp front hooves as well as biting and butting. They will even stand over a fawn when a large bird of prey like a golden eagle approaches.

(above left) Not the most glamorous aspect of pronghorn motherhood, this doe consumes the feces and urine of one of her twin fawns by licking its anal and genital regions. Why? Because its body waste carries a scent, thus providing the only trail a predator can follow to the hidden toddler. Hiding fawns will refrain from defecating until mom returns.

(above right) Only a few days old at most, this little fawn rises from its hiding place as it spots its mother's approach.

(left) A constant menace for the young fawns through much of the summer is the ever-lurking coyote. These cunning and fabled creatures are the chief predator of pronghorn fawns, taking many from each year's crop.

A Cradle in the Grasslands

(above) A doe nurses one of her fawns in a cottonwood grove along a prairie creek during mid-June. Most does breed for the first time when they are about fifteen months old.

(left) After ten days or so, fawns will still recline and hide during the day, but usually do so with their head erect like this one and paying more attention to their surroundings.

(facing page) Even pronghorn mothers get exasperated with their children, like this one that finally snarls at her little doe fawn who insists on more milk. Fawns begin eating vegetation when they are about three weeks old and are usually weaned completely by ten to twelve weeks.

(above) The play of fawns is actually a feature of behavioral development and involves sparring, head butting, and chasing, along with many other activities. Mock battles like this one between two buck fawns are common and can get very aggressive as they learn some of the hierarchical laws of the pronghorn society; injuries are rare.

(right) Having survived the hiding phase and now about twenty days old, this fawn faces a new set of challenges in its development. About this time the mothers bring their young into small social groups comprised of other mothers and fawns where they will spend the next two months or so. Through this time the fawns will be weaned, become fully functional ruminants, and learn something about social ranking among their species.

(facing page) Fast running mixed with occasional leaps and twists are not just antics of childhood play, but are also very important in the locomotive development of this little buck. Games like this one help develop the young legs that will save his life more than once in the years to come. After two or three dashes back and forth over a distance of thirty yards or so, the youngster will simply stand panting.

(above left) *After a few weeks the fawns begin to follow their mothers as they forage. By midsummer they have joined into doe-fawn groups that normally number about a dozen.*

(above right) *Also at about this time, the fawns grow very curious of their surroundings, losing some of their fear of the new and different.*

(right) *Amidst these day-care groups the fawns become fast friends and playmates like these three, teasing and chasing one another through the summer grass.*

(facing page) *Following the intense and vigilant behavior required during the hiding period, the does appear to relax when they bring their fawns into these groups where more eyes and ears provide more security.*

(above) With the combination of rich milk and summer foliage, fawn activity increases dramatically as fawns grow. This little buck dashes about from mother to playmates. By the age of three months he will have acquired the familiar and striking pelage of the adults.

(right) Now starting to grow its first horns, this three-month-old buck fawn enjoys a late summer drink.

(facing page) As a mid-July thunderstorm breaks up, a doe fawn feeds on the rich summer vegetation of a prairie meadow that is rapidly becoming the more dominant aspect of her diet. Generally, females reach their full adult weight at four to five years of age, much later than other ruminants. Researchers continue to debate the reasons for this.

(facing page) By and by, the frolicking fawns return to their mother's dugs for her rich milk described by naturalist John James Audubon as "thick as undiluted evaporated milk, but less sweet." It has twice the protein and more than three times the fat content of a domesticated cow's milk. At about ten weeks old, these fawns are probably in their final days of nursing.

The Rut

(above) Younger bucks like these in a bachelor group of eleven will be a constant source of aggravation for the dominant buck as they circulate his territory or harem, trying to lure away does. Because they "orbit" an area, they are sometimes known as satellite bucks. Males that survive their first winter join a bachelor herd like this one and alternate between the large mixed-sex winter group and summer bachelor herds until they are four to five years old.

(facing page) The rut begins in early September as an intense competition between large mature bucks like this one that employ one of two mating strategies. They mark and defend a specific territory on which no other bucks are permitted or they gather and defend a harem of does among which no other bucks are permitted. Both plans will involve serious confrontations.

Buck Fever

The brawny pronghorn buck leapt to his feet, outraged at the audacity of these intruders who dared violate the sanctity of his clearly marked domain. Raising his proud head, he curled back his lips and began to huff and puff, his entire body rigid like wrought iron. Who were these pugnacious infidels?

Not satisfied with mere protests, the fuming buck broke into a flamboyant prance, slowly encircling the group of five does who continued to feed on the shrubs of this high prairie plateau, apparently indifferent to the new presence. The gatecrashers stood on opposite hilltops, one about 30 yards away, the other about 100 yards off—their intentions were clear and obvious.

Throughout most of the year a pronghorn male lives in a group, either the large mixed-gender groups of winter that can number fifty-plus animals or summer bachelor groups of ten to fifteen.

Come the rut in September things change. Mature or dominant bucks separate from their groups for this intense and very competitive season. Some become territorial bucks. They mark and defend a ground against intrusion from other bucks and claim all does that venture onto it. Others gather a harem of does that they vigorously keep together while excluding other bucks.

Bachelor groups are generally composed of younger animals where the young buck learns the way of things in his society. As the rut begins, some of the "bachelors" become satellite bucks like this morning's invaders, roaming the perimeter of a territorial buck's ground like a satellite orbiting a planet, attempting to steal or lure away members of the harem.

Other species such as elk and bighorn sheep also gather harems, but the pronghorn harem is unique. Normally an elk cow or bighorn ewe will just stand by while the males dispute the question of "ownership" among themselves, accepting the terms of their settlement with little question.

Not so with the pronghorn doe. Having little regard for the male viewpoint, she is going to mate with the biggest and best buck she can find, meaning she will check out all the possibilities, regardless of what her self-appointed master may think. This policy would soon be evident this morning.

Clearly fed up with his competitors, the territorial buck sprang forward and sprinted toward the near trespasser. Reaching the satellite buck, he chased it back up the prairie slope where the two quickly disappeared over the hilltop. The other transgressor realized his opportunity.

In that same flashy style as the territorial buck, he trotted down from the ridge toward a doe that glanced over her shoulder at his approach. Coming to within a few feet of her, he began to wag his head back and forth as he continued his advance, displaying the dark subauricular gland on his lower jaw. If the doe does not turn or walk away, but sniffs at the buck's glands, then she has probably reached estrus and is ready to mate.

As he reached her, the doe trotted ahead a few feet and paused, looking straight ahead and then behind. Again, the buck approached and once more she spurned his advance.

Reappearing on the opposite ridge, the territorial buck saw his dilemma. In what seemed only an instant, he reached the side of the intruder. Both began to paw at the ground, and then the big buck lunged at the younger one, locking antlers with him and shoving him backwards. The young buck gamely tried to hold his

(above) A territorial or site-faithful buck marks his ground by rubbing his subauricular gland, the large black skin patch located on the side of his head at the posterior angle of the jaw against stout and conspicuous plants as a warning to rival bucks. This gland produces several compounds, most notably one called isovaleric acid that leaves a sticky touch and a very pungent odor wherever the buck makes his mark. In addition to subauricular marking, bucks will also paw away a small patch of vegetation and then mark the spot by urinating and defecating on it.

ground, but he was outmatched and was soon overwhelmed. He broke off contact, heading back in the direction from which he had come, with the landlord in close pursuit.

Now came the doe's opportunity. Off she headed in the direction of the other intruder as if such was her plan all along. Oh, so coy.

The territorial buck didn't think so. Whirling about, he flew across the grassland, quickly overtaking the errant doe. The chase was on. Dodging, turning, and sprinting once again, the two were almost a blur as they shot over the prairie, reaching speeds in excess of fifty miles per hour.

The chase was short lived on this hot September morning, and the doe was soon herded back into her "proper place." Again the territorial buck pranced about his harem, declaring his sovereignty with the same flamboyance as before.

The does casually went back to their feeding, though still keeping watch for those intruder bucks, not having put other ideas out of their heads as yet. The territorial buck could be optimistic, but it was plain to see that he was not really in control here. The days ahead would demand continued vigilance.

Who's in charge?

(above) While the buck is credited as being the dominant force in the rut due to his defense of territory or collection of a harem, the important choices are really made by the doe. As shown here, most does routinely reject the advances of young bucks like these three amigos.

(left) A territorial buck refreshes himself with a drink from a small prairie pond before getting on with the business of the rut. Like this buck's ground, the best territory includes adequate food and water, good vantage points for continuous visual scrutiny, and plenty of other pronghorn.

Grasslands Competitors

(above) Chasing down and herding errant does like this one back into his fold is another activity that will keep a dominant buck greatly occupied throughout much of the rut, costing him much expense in energy and fat reserves that will be critical to winter survival. Notice how sharply the doe cuts, even while on a full dash at nearly fifty miles per hour.

(facing page) The early part of the rut is the most intense when battles like this one between a territorial buck (left) and a challenger can get pretty serious, though most occur only when a doe in estrus is immediately present. These dangerous encounters can sometimes result with bucks suffering severe wounds from horn points, including the loss of an eye and even death.

(above) After running off yet another invader, this dominant buck struts around his collection of does while displaying his subauricular glands and sniffing at the air to see if any have reached estrus. He will repeat this process many times over during a typical morning. Narrow and out-of-sight valleys like this one with high vantage points all around are usually where a buck attempts to keep his flock.

(below) Just because these does are hanging together now doesn't mean they will continue to do so.
As with all pronghorn social groups, this harem is a temporary gathering of individuals with weak
bonds and is very fluid in nature, unlike some species where the harem is a cohesive unit of related
females. The does commonly practice mate sampling before making their final selection as they
attempt to check out all possibilities with little regard for the views of any self-appointed master.
This extra step in the selection process helps provide for a stronger animal whose survival chances
are enhanced that much more in an ecosystem known for its climatic extremes and challenges.

(above) Serious fights like this one occur abruptly when one buck lowers his head and the other does not retreat. The animals actually do attempt to gore each other, with each trying to force the other's head down into a vulnerable position. Usually these fights end just as suddenly with one breaking off contact and running away.

(above right) Often in conjunction with scent marking, bucks will vigorously rake their horns through vegetation in a process called thrashing. Afterwards, they will even hold their heads carefully so as not to lose their grassy adornments.

(right) With this buck's final approach, the doe signals that she is in full estrus and ready to mate by licking her lips and standing still. The buck also licks his lips as he moves behind her to mount.

(above) Pronghorn does are in complete control of the courtship sequence. Only after several thwarted attempts is this buck finally able to mount the doe for copulation. The males are actually quite graceful as they mount, but beyond that a pronghorn courtship is hardly the stuff of which romance novels are made, as the copulation act lasts only a few seconds at most.

Supply and Demand

(above) Jousts and battles that carried serious risks only a few weeks before are now mostly a matter of posturing and sparring such as here. After locking horns, these two bucks only turn and twist their heads a bit with no real danger. Harmless play like this is also common among young bucks in bachelor groups as they develop skills for the years to come.

(right) This influx of breeding does has great impact on the established orders of dominance, and young bucks like this one (right) finally get their chance, provided they first pay proper homage to the master as shown here.

(facing page) As the rut continues into late September, does like these that have been nursing fawns all summer have now weaned their young and join the ranks of the available.

(above) Battle scars like the shredded left prong on this buck are the combat medals of the rut, with nearly half the bucks in any given area displaying such wear. But the damage is limited to the keratin sheaths that are shed in early winter and regrown by early spring, completely repaired.

(right) With the mating battles of early fall pretty much forgotten and dominant bucks abandoning their territories and harems, young bucks like these two get comparatively unimpeded opportunities to mate with the growing supply of does. However, the does still don't feel any obligation to the bucks' fantasies or ambitions, as this one quickly spurns the advances of these two "wanabees."

(below) The rut actually ends rather abruptly. Seemingly
overnight, bucks abandon the harems and territories that they
staunchly defended during the last many weeks and join groups
of mixed ages with both genders, staying together through the
winter months. Typically, these herds run in perfect unison in a
very tight and oval-shaped formation, much like a flock of birds.

(above) Snow can sometimes come to the plains as early as October, though it usually doesn't last long. Here a young buck and two does paw the snow to get at the autumn forage.

(above) A buck and doe dash up a hillside in a routine display of their species' implausible speed. Zoologist John Byers of the University of Idaho believes the most compelling reason for the pronghorn's fleetness stems from the presence of a North American cheetah prior to the late Pleistocene extinctions and that today's pronghorn may actually be somewhat slower than those ancient animals.

(left) Pronghorn are largely diurnal, meaning they are most active during daylight hours—mornings and early evenings in particular—like this buck framed by a rising moon.

Epilogue

(above) With the games and frolic of summer now past, winter preparations have instinctively become this buck fawn's main focus and attention as he gorges himself on the shrubs of late autumn.

(left) These sibling fawns, a buck and doe, have beaten the odds with both surviving a dangerous summer of lurking predators. They now sport adult coats and have no trouble keeping pace with any of the adults as they are fully prepared to enter their first winter. Both will spend most of that season in the same winter group as their mother, but the buck will probably join a bachelor group in late winter or early spring.

(above) This deep ravine in Custer State Park will provide great protection for this doe fawn and her kind from frigid blizzards that can drive wind chills to -50 F. or worse on the high plains.

(left) Displaying a broken prong tip sustained during the autumn rut battles, this buck must now shift his priorities to winter survival as the first snows of the changing season usually come in late November on the high plains, where winter's grip can last well into April.

(facing page) Skim ice is already starting to form on the surface of this prairie pond where a doe drinks on a late autumn morning.

A Testament to Resilience

Winter fast approaches on the northern prairies. For all inhabitants, it is a time of preparation and adaptation for the critical time ahead. Many of the prairie's songbirds, shorebirds, and waterfowl have headed south, leaving a strange, unsettling silence across the grasslands. Herbivores like the prairie dog and ground squirrel gather and store food.

Like many, the pronghorn feed furiously to build up fat reserves that will insulate and nourish their bodies through the coming lean and harsh months. But survival is nothing new to an animal that epitomizes success in an ecosystem boasting of harsh extremes. The prairie is indeed a place for survivors.

Survival is really just a numbers game, one that the pronghorn plays and wins. With most births being multiple, pronghorn fecundity ranks among the highest of large mammals. More than once this birthrate has enabled it to quickly recover from natural disasters that have decimated its ranks.

During the particularly severe North American winter of 1985-1986, wind chills of minus 100 degrees blasted the plains of South Dakota, causing nearly eighty percent of the state's pronghorn population to wither and perish. After only five years, the numbers had rebounded to the present 50,000.

The pronghorn also survived the human migration across the North American continent during the 18th and 19th centuries. When Europeans first ventured onto the western prairies, its numbers were about 30 to 40 million. By the early 1920s, largely unchecked commercial hunting had pushed them close to the brink of extinction, numbering only about 13,000. South Dakota's population alone had

fallen from around 1 million to fewer than 700. Today the continental population has recovered to slightly more than 1 million.

The pronghorn's escape from extinction's abyss can largely be attributed to the rise of a new thinking during the early part of the 20th century. We realized that our spacious prairies, majestic mountains, and bountiful forests and their various inhabitants were not simply resources to be used and consumed, but also national treasures to be coveted and cared for.

(above) Watching this buck routinely munch on the pad of a prickly pear cactus adds further testimony to the pronghorn's tenacity for survival.

(Left) The snow-filled grasslands can actually provide camouflage cover for the pronghorn with his brown tones similar to those of the dried winter grass and his whites like snow. They are also the only large mammal of the North American prairie with a broken pattern coat.

(above) Living on dry and dead foliage like this is only one of many adaptations made by this yearling buck while surviving his first winter on the prairie.

(left) Winter survival is nothing new or complicated for an animal that evolved during an ice age. As she feeds among other pronghorn on a cold and snowy morning, this doe is already pregnant again and will have little trouble surviving the season on this meager fare. Her gestation period will even extend if the winter is particularly severe, with the doe probably giving birth to twin fawns during the latter part of May or early June.

(facing page) During winter, resting or reclining pronghorn will generally select a downward slope and orient the longitudinal axis of their body so that their backs are usually to the north with their anterior downwind from extreme chill factors. Depending on where they live, some pronghorn will migrate from summer ranges to winter ranges to better take advantage of available and nutritious forage. In and around South Dakota's Black Hills, they do not need to migrate because the land has plenty of food all year long.

(above) Midwinter snows encase the dried grasses of the previous summer across this rolling South Dakota prairie lit by soft sunlight at the end of a very cold January day. Ravines like this one were carved by the glacial movements of the last ice age a few million years ago when the pronghorn that we know today began to evolve and emerge from its Old World ancestors.

(above) Pronghorn skin is richly supplied with blood vessels that facilitate the growth of more hairs per square inch across their bodies during winter. A thick pelage is formed with an outer layer of hollow, air-filled hairs that provide excellent insulation from the extreme cold of Arctic air blasts that frequent the northern plains.

(right) The mixed-gender groups of winter tend to feed on hillside slopes like this one. Frequently swept by winds, the foliage here is kept free of packed snow and accessible to the pronghorn. Most important to them at this time of year are shrubs like sagebrush and western snowberry. These woody plants survive from year to year with over-wintering parts that are above ground. Pronghorn are also adept at pawing aside snow to uncover edible foliage.

(above) Two mature bucks keep a watchful vigil on the outer perimeter of their winter group as they safeguard against the approach of predators during the breakup of a snowstorm.

(right) During heavy snowfalls, pronghorn like this yearling doe will generally opt for habitats around groves of trees along creek banks where snow gathers least, thus easing the difficulties of winter foraging.

It would be wrong to assume that the pronghorn is an icon of the prairie that will always be with us. Other great beasts have been pushed aside. Bison live today only in small fragments of their former numbers. Creatures like the grizzly bear, elk, and cougar that were once as much a part of the prairie fauna as the pronghorn have largely been exiled to remote mountain habitats and northern wildernesses where they exist in mere token numbers when compared to the past. And the pronghorn are too singularly adapted to the prairie to go anywhere else.

Only the continued efforts and cooperation within a network of landowners, conservationists, hunters, professional managers, and enthusiasts can ensure that the pronghorn will remain in its realm.

An award-winning photojournalist and nature photographer, Dick Kettlewell shares his passion for the landscapes and wildlife of the North American prairie from his home near Custer State Park in South Dakota.